endorsements

At once a tirade against thieves and a spell for healing cast over the self, Olivia Laughlin's *The Size of Mars* wades through planetary grief to arrive, at last, at possibility. In Olivia's poetic voice, sadness is not a state to overcome, but a prism to be shone through: she is both a "sad miracle," and a body "equipped to keep living." Through the fog of mourning, Olivia's poems point a way.

- Emmanuel Oppong-Yeboah, *City of Boston Poet Laureate*

The Size of Mars reads like a wound learning how to speak. Olivia Laughlin writes with a tenderness that burns—each poem a match struck against silence, each image a hand reaching through the dark. Her words carry the weight of what was taken and the grace of what was reclaimed, mapping grief not as an ending but as a threshold. Paired with her artwork, this collection becomes a living room of ash and light, where heartbreak is honored, survival is sanctified, and becoming feels possible again.

My favorite piece, *the August that burnt the house down*, is a devastating masterwork—love rendered as theft, the body as an unlocked home, grief as both ash and awakening. It is an unforgettable meditation on what we give away, what is taken from us, and the fierce, hard-won clarity that arrives when we finally learn what love is not. This is a book that doesn't just hold you—it teaches you how to hold yourself.

- Amanda Shea, *3x Spoken Word Artist of the Year by the Boston Music Awards*

Olivia Laughlin's poetry stopped me in my tracks. Page after page, I found myself whispering damn as her lines carved straight into the bone. Her work is potent, unflinching, and haunting. Her artwork adds a beautiful depth to her poems.

She writes about heartbreak with a softness that still stings, capturing how love can color a season and then leave you standing in the ruins of your own longing. She writes emotional devastation with striking clarity, turning ordinary moments into mirrors that reveal everything we try to hide from ourselves. Her poems hold the ache of memory, the tension of trying to save the parts of ourselves that still believe in love, and the quiet bravery of choosing to rebuild.

And when she turns her pen toward the world, the impact is shattering. I cried as she peeled back the layers of injustice, privilege, grief, and collective suffering with a holy rage and trembling honesty in American Crime Story. She refuses to let the reader look away from the truth and somehow still offers the possibility of a world remade through courage and compassion.

This collection is a reckoning. Olivia Laughlin writes with precision, power, and a voice that lingers. Anyone who encounters this book will leave transformed.

- SublimeLuv (@QueenSublimeLuv), *LA Spoken Word Artist*

The Size of Mars

Olivia Laughlin

MERAKI PRESS

Paperback ISBN: 979-8-9991650-1-5

Cover Image: Olivia Laughlin
Cover Design and Layout: Katie Zeliger
Artwork: Olivia Laughlin

Printed in the United States of America
Meraki Press LLC
www.merakipress.org

First Edition

To my sisters,
Brianna and Julia.
Thank you for helping me survive everything that turned into this book.

table of contents

table of contents

preface

the journey to your hands
has brushed soil and sky
these pages
have climbed their way
out of sealed ground
poetry is the legs
the sharpened lip of the shovel
the revived green in the grass
the airborn wing
poetry is the plea to stay

the collapse

I saw in the news
the spine of the structure
crumbled not long after I left,
that it collapsed into dust
no natural disaster needed
karma was already on her way to you
and it sickened you like a snapped muscle
detached in the lost sea of the body
they said
the windows shot into a thousand knives
left your heart pierced and vulnerable
what an odd coincidence
my revenge was never needed
I only mattered to you once your bedroom was an organ gutted raw
dresser gaped open, decay on the door hinges
I mattered once her body felt like an abandoned church
a song you no longer knew the words to
a prayer that never made it past your knuckles

the time traveler

I pour poems
in your coffee
mornings at a time
everything feels like photosynthesis sticking to the pads of my palms
your hands turn to amusement parks after dark
I tell you I want to make a movie about your life
I mean that
being with you feels like time-traveling
early two thousands crackling through the stereo
the sting of tequila in the parking lot
enmeshing in a crowd of tilting chins
all admiring your stature coating the stage
we are dreamers but don't sleep much these days
I watch you drive around town after the show
singing memories into the sky
the morning sun seeping through open windows
skydiving off your stories
you ask me to sing for you
I press the breeze against my forehead
I put love on my tongue
I open my mouth
you look at me like a miracle everytime

bleach

I unweave blonde hairs out of your blanket
and we don't talk about the look on my face
the corners of my mouth crescent to my jawline
my black hair falling over the dew christening my cheeks
we just throw the moon back into the sky
dance around the foundation smeared into your shirt collar
I fall asleep to the sound machine humming over the questions
I'm not allowed to ask
I let the shadows lose their balance
pretend I did not see your eyes shutter
when I asked if there was someone else

February

your valentine's day gift / still waiting /
in my closet wrapped / unopened / you should've come back /
for me / but one month / turned to four / I think about burning /
the gift / that night / I thought maybe / he's buying me flowers /
maybe / that's why / your phone went to voicemail /
but it was her voice / intoxicating your ear / her voice / that answered my call /
her laugh /
as I wept / for you / like a fool / lost in love / telling my friends /
you weren't a bad guy / painting your faults / gold / just for you to /
rust / by February / abandoning myself / just to be abandoned by you too /

I-95 North

I spend the car ride home
singing lullabies to my anxiety
I hold the goodbye deep in my bladder
bite my tongue so the highway won't persuade me
I spend the car ride home
with a hundred knots in my stomach
and a hundred tears down my face
a hundred more knocking on the door
of my thundering thoughts
your secrets like a scratched CD
skipping in my mind
an electrocuting truth
you are in the driver's seat
successfully ignoring the ringworm
in my breathing
I turn to you for the first time
in an hour
and I made you look at my face
the rivers you placed in my tear ducts
I made you look at the hurt you promised
you'd protect me from
you tell me to write a poem
that was the best gift
you ever gave to me
I have not stopped
writing poems about
the slow-motion murder of my hope in you
I often wonder
how many years my mind
will live in that passenger seat
how many times I will take a different way home
just to end up in the memory of your arms
how long will it take
for that car ride to end

April's fool
the poem I wrote that day

Dear   April
                              I've   rained
          as   much   as   you   told   me   not   to
                  every   night   i   have   nightmares
that   leave me
sleep walking
                  into   the   attic
and   i   don't   miss   you
                                          i   miss   the   parts   of   me
That   used   to   paint   peonies   on the walls
Now   i am in   the   dust ridden corners   of   my   mind
                  no longer sacred
                              with these picked   locks
Everything   the   thieves   have   taken
                                    i   handed   to   them
April,
                              I   have   hope
but the insulation is thinning in my words
there's conditional love in my cereal
i harvest myself flowers while   i'm   still   alive

dear april
i am tired of the dust mites

dear april
how many days until May?

the size of Mars

I try to write poems about you
....
but
the words start
crying off the page.........................
you remain a poison
I dispense every morning
....
you are building houses
....
in the middle.............of my sentences
smearing caramel.........................
all over the clock's hands
slowing down the distance
I try to put between
me... and you
making midnight miss the motion sickness
of our spontaneous summer
giving the flashbacks a backbone
....................................a pocket knife to their death
a stain on the page.........................
a silhouette to sit next to your grave
a grief the size of   m   a   r   s

the body spit out

my tears know what it looks like to run
back to the source
the body who bred the demons
the body who slayed them
in the same lifetime
the tears always take her by surprise
so she and body
lay in the middle of a field
fall in love with pink clouds
declare my bed unholy ground
some days my humanness strips me dry
some days the tears are so silent
I mistake myself for your secrets
the world can fall apart anywhere
the world has lost limbs inside me
I spend the night fishing for parts of you
trying to convince parts of me
to stay in broken places
you want me to be silent as plates shift beneath our crust
to let the earth erode inside me
and pronounce it love
you wave goodbye to my body
try to scare the tears into silence
so spit it out
call it mutiny
we both know
I never asked for anything in return

king, your eyelids
e windshield
. Tear glands in
ers of your

and
them
ps the
your
clean.
controlled
automatic
esides working
utomatic control

Tear gland

after the tone

the missed phone calls
are strung across the floor
flailing into an abyss
your number is blocked
but your silence gyrates my eardrums
I can feel the lack of war
and your pride shushing my memory
a lullaby on a battlefield
mask molded to your cheek bones
I wish you were spinning, too
like every room I walk into
but the truth is
whether you know it or not
there is no other me
you will not find me in another woman's body
you will not forget
how my magic put all the swords to rest

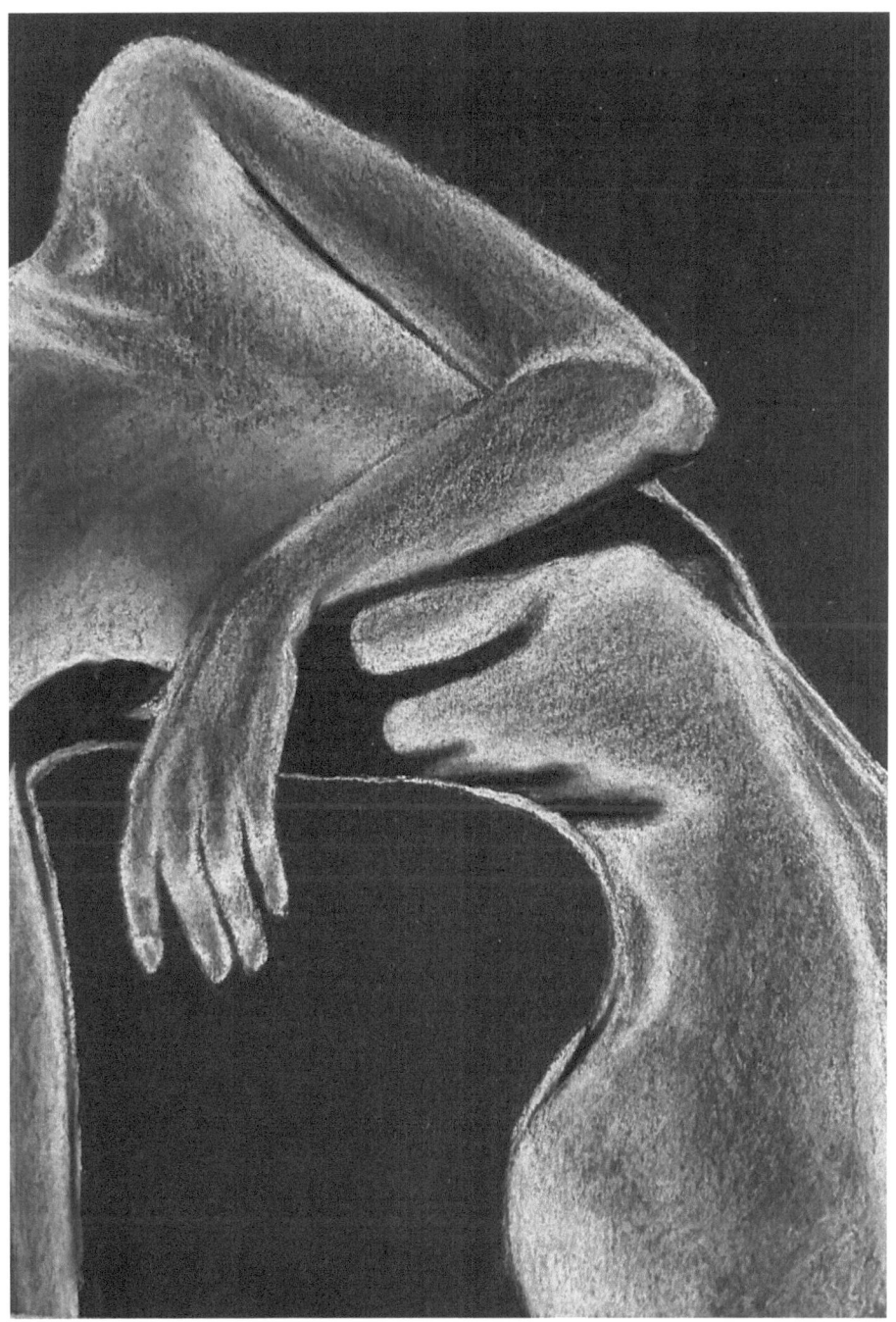

do I mean anything to myself now that I mean nothing to you
will my skin slip off the bone because you held me with filthy hands
because our story has the aftertaste of another woman's home

the maroon trail

you watched your woman
light the match on my skin
heard the cry crack through my lungs
did you forget my flammability?
that night, did you give her the flowers
I asked for?
did they smell like a funeral when they burned?
are they rotting through the bedroom walls?
tell me, have they stained her skin?
does the house feel haunted now?

flight delayed

I tell the butterflies in my stomach
to go back to bed
the boy is a dragon
the sky is still polluted
a monarch can't survive here
it is still not safe to fly

false alarm

the way you look at me makes me feel like less of a miracle

I hang four versions of my body on the wall
let you pick your favorite
we never agree on the same one
but to be chosen at all these days
is better than to be left hanging

tongue-twister

love was never your
native tongue it was pride from
that coarse ego

wasn't it?

July on Olive Street

July's fireworks
spoiled on the lawn

how badly I did not want to watch
another summer romance

become a mistake
how slowly the sun emptied from my eyes

I chose you before knowing you
seeing you in all types of rooms

you'd never make it into
walking where midnight lives

burning red in a black ocean
the starless sky pitying my efforts

I remember everything about everyone who has ever held me
I am a well of fragmented love stories

will the color orange remember me once I'm covered in blue
how many sunsets do I have left

my tongue folded over yours and
I tasted the sweetest July

by the end of the month goodbye coats my gums
slips off my teeth and onto your bronzed shoulders

a memorized rhythm of the tongue
you would not say my name

what kind of person did I become
leaving myself for the birds

I am a palette of pastels blended seamless in the clouds
I am every summer sunset I could not find in you

did my abundance blind you
I expect love because I am made of it

I walk around believing in it
tell me, how do I kill that part of myself?

I am made of the softest tendon
I have all this love left

I hold it tight to my chest
saving every last bit for myself

thirst

　　　　it doesn't matter
how many times
　　　　he brings you flowers
　　if
he doesn't water
　　　　the ones in you

22

the compliments were the gateway drugs to come inside

you take my body
leave my magic on the side table
everything I've spent centuries
fructifying into fluorescence
lays dormant under a pile of clothing
showing interest
was just your entrance plan

growing pains

thank you for giving
up on me. I had no choice
but to grow new legs

in the placcs you lived
thank you for leaving
so the best of me could stay alive

a walk on water

I was made from a tired God
one who left a type of heaven in my hands
Sunday syrup
dry by sundown
sticky in syllables
my joy
a swelling of song
an unpronounced ending
nesting in beginning
Noah's ark
back bending over molasses river
new moon baptism
three lives in one body
when she arrives
all of us walk on water
this heaven can be burned time and time again
and still rise as a branding of rebirth

how do you learn to love again
when you've only ever lost yourself to it

letters from Gloucester

there was a pile of unburned love letters
rearranging themselves into your eulogy
no one else feels like you
that was supposed to be a good thing
I miss you
like body folding into prayer
an auditorium of clasped joints
swaying in the middle of the high tide
the Atlantic in my lungs
my frame forgoing the breast stroke
your scent walks into every room I've run into
I grow gills
diving into vessels
searching for your skin in theirs
I miss you
even as I escape the inflamed home
even as I scrape the paint off the walls
and unravel your front door from my ribs
as I remember you in crumbs
I pretend the fire didn't start that Friday
I remember you as the man
I always made up in my head
I stretch out that one night like we were always made of lasting devotion

goodbye is a run-on sentence

my mind
plays the movie of us
a thousand times
I've memorized
the sounds of your existence
I've created
a whole planet that
reminds me of you

under a red sun

I carry rocks from under your bed
all the way home
believing the weight is mine
convinced if I carry them long enough
the rocks will turn to sand
the shoreline laughs at me
"that was never your job"

last week my therapist said to me:
"it's not your fault, the way they've treated you.
their unkindness is not your weight to carry"

sugar drought

I let your memory sear in the sun
the image of us belly laughing on the living room floor
now frying to charcoal on the sidewalk
I watch the sugar evaporate
let the heat steal all its sweetness
what is left is
the knocking on your apartment door
our ending perched in the peep hole
splenda packets punctured
you no longer hold this soft space inside me
now my nose twists when I think of you
salt singes my sinuses
I kill the version of me that stooped so low
to love you enough
to lose me

crimson

the boy opens his hands
to show his innocence
one day he is clover, the next crimson
Monday wraps me
in peach colored blush
flowering my cheeks in morning kisses
Tuesday steps on my skin
with cleats
leaves my pores congested with mud
my body regresses
into a revolving door
he leaves and enters
at his convenience
he does not ask
if he can use my body
as a foot stool
if he can hurt my body
he just sinks his feet in
splits me under his weight
doesn't bother
to sew me back up
once he's done

the bending of a woman

I don't remember how to dance alone
since I bent myself into an option for you
I trip over myself trying to remember how to waltz
waist paralyzed by your purgery
puppeted plié
I don't remember conversations with training wheels
there was no introduction
no time for the "no" to make it out of my body alive
just bare flesh before bone
splayed limb across the queen mattress
the sawdust eroded on the cotton sheets
you destructing my outsides
to get to my insides
me, rehearsing the word "no" in the mirror
for the next month

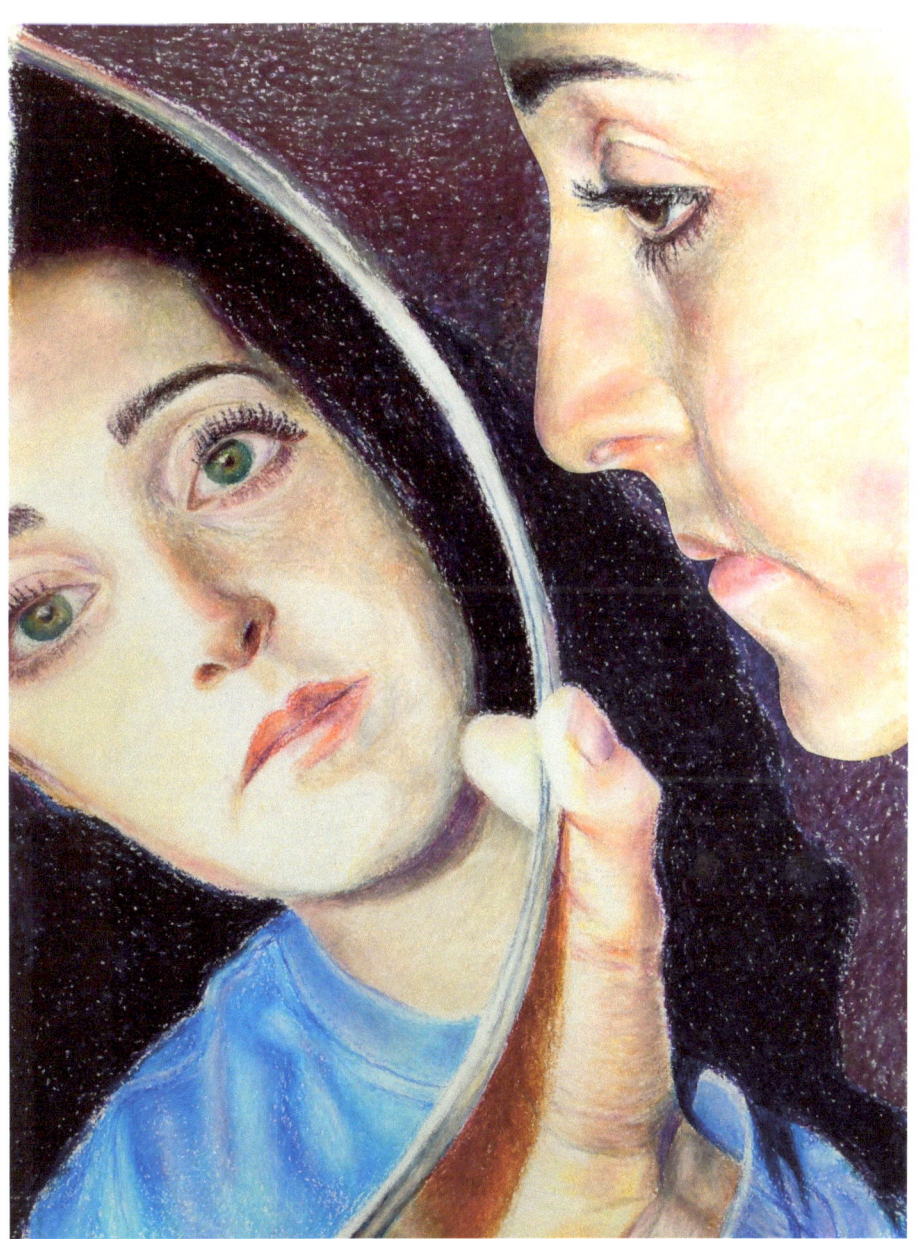

Neptune's curse

yesterday,
I saw your ghost dancing in the living room
spent an hour scrubbing your silhouette off the walls
you were never made of the same material as me
you were the farthest planet from the sun

yesterday,
I saw your ghost dancing in the living room
playing fetch with the cobwebs
I am tired of mourning you
the way Neptune dreams of bathing in sunlight

yesterday,
I saw your ghost dancing in the living room
I let you dance until you fatigued
let your outline blur to ambiguity
let the moon slowly tear the truth out of you

reminders

I see you everywhere
today, you are the landscaper
sunburnt eyelids
sliced grass sticking to your perspiration
tomorrow, you are the broken blinker
infecting the intersection
leading me to dead ends
yesterday, you were the dirty bed sheets
the detergent keeps sliding off
I've cut my arms off a million times
just to stop them from reaching for you
still you are a stubborn phantom limb
I keep having to convince myself
is gone for good

manhunt

I am a season skinned alive
the zing in the barrel of a gun
lining the shore in bullet fragments
I am less and less of myself
I lose my arm on tuesday
my leg in the spring
I build mountains out of bodies
lost inside me
I am the hoax I've hated
I am hollow hallelujah
you break me down until I am
bite sized
gunpowder
made me a weapon
no tears, all teacher
no safety, all trigger
a lesson learned the long way

swimming lessons

today I watch a body
crawl down the drain
hands swallow themselves
into apologies
you are always making yourself into
a sink hole for someone else
now the moon is melting down the walls
and the bath is overflowing through the kitchen ceiling
the chairs are floating
the house doesn't know how to swim
and you still can't let anyone in

pulling strings

my body is not the most important thing about me
I'm still trying to convince myself of this truth

do you know how hard it is to breathe
when everyone loves to see a woman hold her breath

the night you left

the ceiling collapsed last night
and I didn't notice

        I sang a song with my tongue cut out
        and couldn't hear the difference

I ran through the streets for you
at 5am

        a blinking traffic light
        my clamoring body

        I stripped the stars from the sky
        gutted the clouds

refurbished the rain
became nothing for you

        clawed my eyes out
        I planted the seeds of a new language for you

became an entrance mat in a fully furnished house
shapeshifted myself into a skeleton for you

        but you never came back

Dear July

a jaguar got my tongue
shredded it to mush
gourged me to a rind
got blood all over the carpet
I didn't tell you where I was last week
you wouldn't have cleaned up the mess
would've watched as I scaled the wooden floor
army crawled to the phone

Dear July
it was a Tuesday when they sat me down
their words, a heat wave in my living room
they told me what Nantucket saw you do
you thought the tide would wash it away
that night it took a bite out of my thigh
fourth of July fireworks
running rabid down the walls of my apartment
burning me from both ends

Dear July
I waited by the phone
hypnotised by the blue light
clenched my jaw until my molars flattened
no missed calls
people stop checking on crybabies
because we flood houses
you couldn't save the furniture and save me too

Dear July
why do you prey on me in the season that holds the most daylight

Dear July
incoherency fogs the wait room
the walls are a sticky gray
the woman whose name tag says Jillian pulls out a camera
apologizes, *"we need a picture for identification purposes"*
I drag my knuckles across my cheeks
swipe away the nights damage
stare into the lens pushing my quivering lip to my teeth

"thank you dear"
I curl back into my knees as the intake questions clot in my ears

Dear July
the nurse in pink scrubs sits at my bedside
admits the first night is the hardest
feeds me white pills that droop my eyelids to a half moon
says they should make the crying stop long enough for sleep to take me
she told me last Christmas was her July
told me by Easter she could breathe again
told me August things will feel lighter
I tell her I can't wait that long

Dear July
I wake up to the tissue under my eyes speckled with red bursted blood vessels
they put my belongings in a white laundry basket
spelled my name wrong on the label tag
the dressers have rounded edges, the tvs have no hanging cords
dinner is at 4:30

July you took my seat at the table
I stomach two bites of a sour apple
and taste all the summers before this

July
I wish I could spit you out but you are fossilized in my gut

July
can you love me here
with sickness running down my cheek

July
will you claim me like a priest pronounces the last verse of an exorcism
tear the depression from the cavity of my chest
say me loud like your tongue was meant to coil in the shape of my name
watch as I blister, love me anyway

July you didn't even try

July
do you keep me alive for entertainment?
do I make a better poet on my knees?

42

Dear July
they are discharging me today
before I go, the nurse wraps me in her arms
cradles my head and whispers "good luck out there baby girl"

Dear July
will you save next summer for me
will you someday keep me safe

Dear August
can you walk me home now?

the night I left

you were in a crowd of men calling me crazy
as I stood in the middle of the road
you laid beside me hours earlier,
now her body replaced mine
you said you wouldn't
a familiar fatality
you watched my eyes beg
ruptured into shell
acted like I was a stranger
laughing at a girl gone mad
your friends hold their hunching bellies
slap each others chests
follow your lead
cackling and pointing
at the natural disaster
the sprained knees
twisting on the pavement
never thought you'd become the antagonist
in the story I lived a thousand times before you
the wheels of my car scream out of the driveway
you watch as I swerve the mailbox
head in hand
soaking the steering wheel
you never called to see if I made it home
never visited me when you found out I hadn't
left me to teethe on the hospital gown like a sugar cube
dizzy to the sound of the doctor
dissecting my drunken recollection
your wild tongue on a battery
gasoline splashing out your sides
laughing as I burn,
your mouth full of matches

American Crime Story

I have had the privilege of loving and losing
gifted the grace of health, community and resources
to rebuild myself after devastation
while across the world there are people mourning clean water
children dreaming of making it to their next birthday
I break for these realities
and that too is a privilege
to watch the despair from a distance
and have the option of looking away

my tax dollars form spoon to feed the greed
watch it balloon over the sides of its throne
charring the skin of the US dollar
staining the tap water red
I think of Palestinians drinking puddle water
how the Congo cannot crystallize their own cobalt
I wonder how many springs until the Sudanese people can sleep again?
how many borders does an immigrant need
to scrape himself across until he can start hanging
pictures on the walls of his bedroom?
every scream is made of the same lung
I press my ear to the grass as our soils whisper what little can escape
past greed's tightening grip around our windpipe
I shiver when America speaks
gluttony is a deafening sound
signing love letters on missiles that kiss the skies before they bury legacies
cracking the crust of sacred land
littering the flag in blood
how much blood did my freedom cost?
tell me what kind of freedom turns a blind eye to my sisters' and brothers'
endings?
how can I be free
when Haiti is bleeding,
when CEOs are buying yachts while the sick empty their wallets trying to
afford healthcare?

when our police officers disappear Black and Brown bodies behind jail cells?
America wades in convenient delusion
freedom is a word found on the white man's tongue
his freedom stands on the backs of those who built this country
those with complexions the color of cinnamon
America does not learn the names of its victims
will not let their mothers know they won't be coming home
America shames sexual assault survivors into silence
because God forbid a man's reputation is tainted
his whole life would be ruined
he could even become the president of the United States
I will lift the rug every survivor's story was swept under
America will be covered in dust
I refuse to desensitize myself to obscenity
I will continue to let my heart gnaw at each loss
I will build a different world, one home at a time
each brick forged with holy rage
I will believe in a different world
strip the wool off a lying tongue
I will sink it to the ground
I will sing the rage all the way to the white house
let them know we're coming
let them know the matches they light
will brand America

ladylike

he was the straw
that broke the woman's back
what is left
after forest fire
is depleted soil
angry oxygen
homicidal clouds
witnessing the war between four walls
and you expect me to keep composure
you expect repeated trespassing
to be met with politeness
you reprimand the monster you made me
they always want women to swallow war silently
but this time
the syllables are bullets
loading my tongue
I am too triggered to tame

ar·mour[ˈɑːmə]

armor (noun)

1.the metal coverings formerly worn to protect the body in battle:

he says
stop writing poems about me
I laugh
and say
I will stop
when you stop treating bodies like batteries
when the trauma forgets my address
poems are the steel armor
flooding to my rescue
recharging my faith in divine redirection

maybe you should've chosen more wisely
than to tread so carelessly on a poet's skin

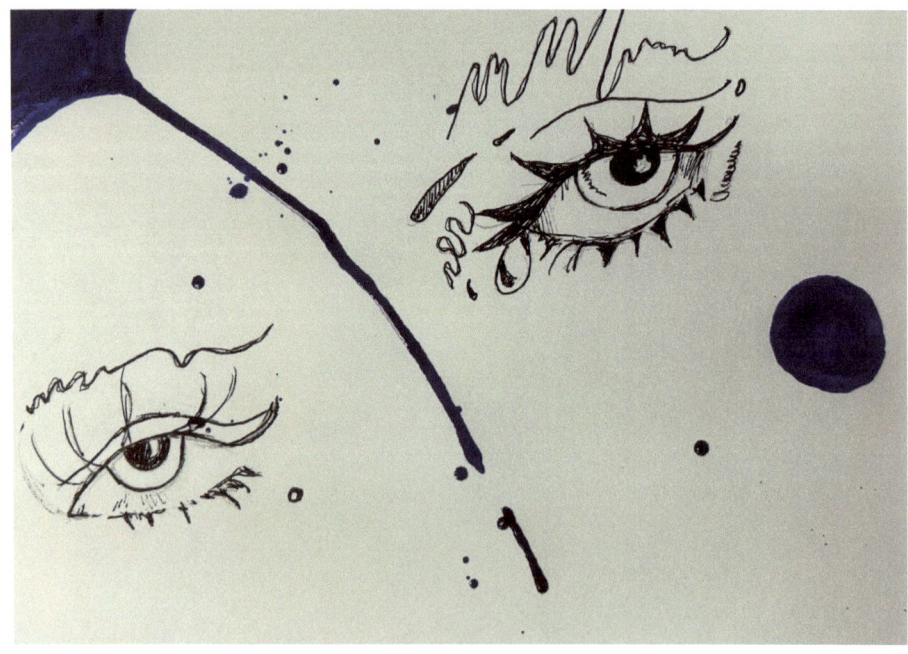

11:11

I wish you a safe trip home
I wish you the arms
to hold all the heavy in you
I hope you end up in that place in the sun
the one that cups the side of your cheek and
leaves cherry kisses on your forehead scar
maybe that's why you let the shower water run
maybe that's why it never bothered you to live somewhere between spring and
summer
where morning dew pools in the rose pedals
swirling their roots through the gaps in your teeth
where you let the woman in you scream
and you can finally be free

do you still live on Stone Lane?

i hope the future is full of melting glass when you get there. hope you make a vase out of the stretching blues rooting the flame. hope you fill it with wildflowers. like you filled me. hope you snip the flower stems diagonally. let them drink. like how my flesh was open. hope the bed you sleep in is the same one you fall in love in. i hope there are succulents on the coffee table. hope you turn the lights on in the room you take your mask off in. i hope they double seal the windows that house your wishes. i hope you come back. not out of convenience, but out of a holy need. i hope i'm not a phase but if i am you haven't phased me. i lie to myself to get through the winter. i'm whispering symptoms of you into the oncoming spring but i'm living the present without your word. cannot admit I'm waiting. i wonder. are you on the other side of the conversation. unsticking the disconnected phone calls from your face. waiting for me to crawl back first. for the clock's hands to meet us in the middle this time.

you never really amazed me anyway

your memory
like the concave of pluto's underbelly
raindrops
evaporated to drought by morning
your absence is tasteless

write these poems for her
write them until she hears you

Milky Way

i.
honeydew enchantment
she is a metallic star
goosebumps coated in
poetic skin

ii.
softness
too fragile for most
softness
her superpower
a skyscraper
in the right hands

iii.
museum eyes
singing to the tie-dye sky
have you ever tasted the Milky Way?

transplant

I'll let you miss me
I'll let the space between us feel heavy
let our love grow mold
I'll take one hundred showers
in hopes my skin forgets your scent
hoping I can pulverize the promises you left
let the wind feast on your granules
hoping I can trade out this heart
for one that never found catharsis in the pillow of your chest

grenades

i.

I balance you on my teeth
not quite ready to burn my tongue
on uncertainty

bottled up daydreams
leaving liquor in my bones
every movement is a drunken alter ego

I pretend tomorrow
is my dance partner
like spinning in circles will leave you in yesterday

too many nights left
empty pillows in my mornings
pancake mix staling in the back of the pantry

cutting planks like waterlogged firewood
that lay dead at hungry flames
no good at what it was cut down for
....

ii.

my skin is on fire
thirsty for a love I've never known
eager to give it out like gold

drink it down like stardust
be a poet under a blue moon
floating in the arms of an endless muse

instead I am parched
burning with a love that has nowhere to go
all my life it's been recoiling back down my throat

to hide inside me
and wait
for something I've convinced myself

will never come
for protective purposes
the stories

that make me sick
live out their lives
loudly in my head

I write poems
to their death
I put periods

where they took breaths
one day at a time
I am taking my mind back

I am throwing grenades in
rooms
once gluttonous with ghosts

where are you now that I need you?

I'm rewriting our memories
marrying the sugar with salt
the roses with roadkill
painting your prose
black and white
the colors came at a cost
loving your light
dismissing your dark
I lost myself to it
so I'm rewriting our memories
letting the muddy waters
clear
if you are
who you say you are
why aren't you still here?

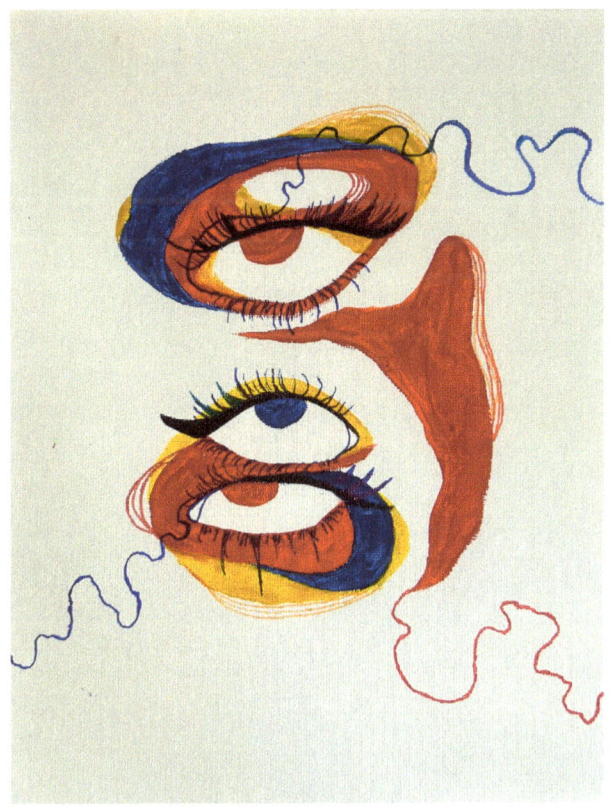

dirty sheets

I don't think I ever admitted to myself
how much it hurts
to picture you
going home to her after you're done with me
how your hands
were calloused from the infidelity
how I felt like a failure
when you touched me
because you tasted like
another woman's home
recycled promises
rehearsed seduction

what is the value of a placeholder
to a homeowner?

i
was so soft
in your hands
and you turned
me to charcoal lungs
gravel palms
stained glass
now the locks don't work

"I was so soft in your hands
and you turned me to charcoal lungs
gravel palms
stained glass
now the locks don't work"

Suzan

the lady in the library
asks me how I'm doing
I spill over
some days I am everything
I am gold in the center of the fire
unburned, unmelted
other days
I am a dying flame
I tell her I am still coughing
up the past year
nursing myself back to life
baptizing my skin in moonlight
she asks me how I'm doing
and I rip splinters from my lips
she asks me how I'm doing
and the whole library lights on fire
I say,
do you know how fire sleeps
burning down to embers
to kindling
uncomfortably alive

I
  will
      not
          apologize
                    for
                       surviving
          earthquakes

by
   becoming
            one.

the only way home

the night you forgot how to love me
the shooting stars stopped falling
from the trees, no chest compressions
could save my fractured organ
I stole my name from your mouth
no longer convincing
itself to live there
I teach you how to pronounce my absence
silence you to this proclamation
you do not have to love me
I'll find my own way home
to a shoreline that tastes like marmalade
I will find a love that keeps
for now I belong to myself
I am my only way home

daydreaming

I want to hang paintings
all over the dining room
of your torso
I want a light show
to waltz between our fingers
watch hope fly from our hallelujahs
I want to be so human
and for you to call it art
I want to find you in every lifetime
and fall in love with every suit of skin
your soul will ever wear
I want to tell you I love you
until it sounds like coming home

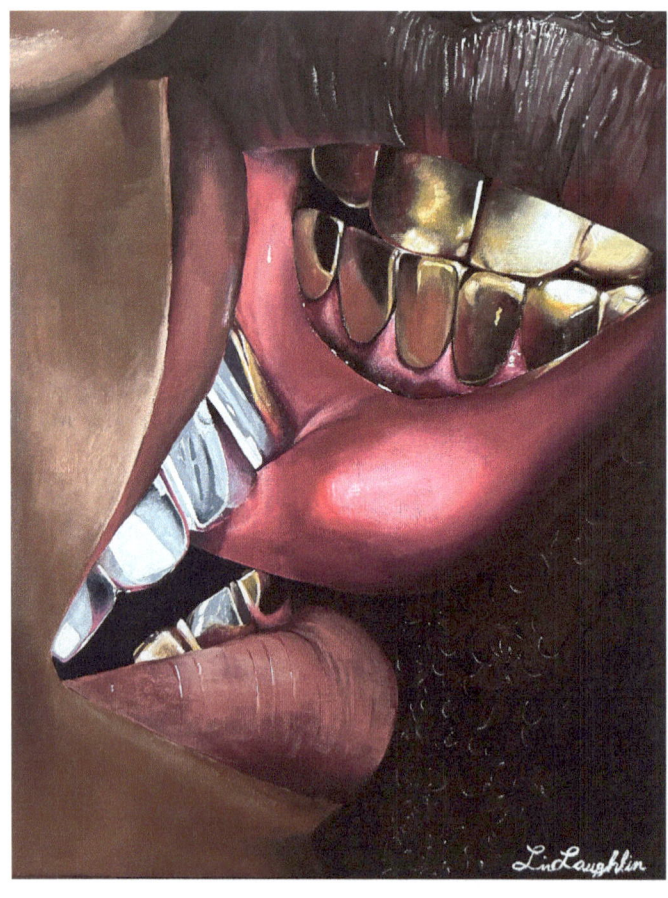

the art of untying knots

suicide and I are no longer friends
I see her sometimes
but her narrative dissipates under my wrath
I unlearned how to kill myself
the noose will no longer stay knotted
I can't stop myself from getting out of bed
I romanticize the future
embrace the version of me who makes it there
the oxygen keeps having baby showers
for all the new ways I've learned
to keep breathing

treading water

you used to tell me
there were no clouds in the sky of our love
with you, it would never rain
when it started pouring in my eyes
I learned to drown for you
do you remember what you said
when the road to you became a river?
you never learned to swim
I could not keep us both
afloat
losing you was my breakthrough
what would you say now
if I told you all about the sun
that was born
the day I left you

why flowers face the sun

for seven months
the walls were sick
black mold spores in every morning's breath
when I wasn't suffering
I was sleeping the year away
this year I rested
swept the underworld of the canyons
saw days with light bulb shards
confettied across the room
I wrote myself into the next day
I wrote myself into a different kind of light
massaged the knots out of my tongue
so I could tell my story in first person
broke down the wall so I could face the sun

the August that burnt the house down

i.
this past August, the house burnt down
the first thing the thieves took was my breath
I never got it back
my first love said he loved me back
when I started gasping for air
I exchanged oxygen for love that day
thought I could only have one
after the robbery I had neither
just a violated body
a vacant room, barren lungs

ii.
the next thief taught me how to tango
before he twisted my body into a toy
and played me until I was blind
I didn't notice the curtains
he draped from my collar bone were stolen
the night I came home to the bed sheets
littered in blonde hair
me, a stolen mannequin in a larcenous museum
that's when I took back his house key
changed my address
saged the new home
unknowingly

iii.
preparing for the next robber
to plant a garden in my backyard
it took months for the seeds to bloom
I used all the water in my body to stir them from the soil
serenaded the sun out from the clouds on every rainy day
until one day the roses stretched their petals outward
and dozens of flowers sprouted simultaneously

iv.
one afternoon in August, all the flowers were clipped
I waited for a bouquet to end up on the kitchen table
but that night I came home to

69

the windows spitting themselves out
a house fire feasting on the living room
a puddle of smoke filling the sky
I followed the trail of gasoline back to him
who had my bouquet in one hand
another woman in the other
the house was gone
my spine corroded
my limbs drowned in asphalt
how long I stayed on my knees in that street
blood started replacing my tears

v.
for the next month, I laid in a pile of ashes
that used to be
the body where I lived
I laid there wondering why
I always left the door unlocked
when every key eventually grew into a stranger
I let them sleep on all the couches
wipe their shoes on my cheeks as they entered
as I watered the gardens they planted for other women
there was always another woman

vi.
love never lived in my house
love does not watch your face become a cave
love does not hang up the phone when you're pouring
love was supposed to come home that night
love should lock the doors
love does not devastate you and still expect
the same version of you to live on

vii.
I cannot call these thieves lovers
and I cannot call these lovers thieves
when I opened the door for them
and told them it was home

"there was a fire last night
you taught me
how to tango
as you twisted
my body into
a toy that you played"

la luz

I hope to rise and fall with the daylight
let my dark come out when it needs to breathe
I hope to lap my demons
I hope to find a wild love
that pulls poems from my skin
and warmth from the safe beneath my ribs
I hope to hold my own hand when people disappoint me
I hope to never take anything too personally
the meteors needed somewhere to land
and I survived each one
I hope to bathe in the suds of sweet tea
I hope I outlaugh my tears
I hope to be so human
this life never outlives me

to do list

1. hold me until
2. the moon is sunny side up again
3. my stomach stops growling
4. for him
5. hold me when
6. I say nothing's left
7. I'm lying
8. remember when
9. the world ended
10. a million times
11. so I created a new one
12. who says
13. I can't do it again

Dear August

you left your stinger in me
I was a bouquet before you
you used to just be my father's birth month
the last note of summer
now you are the start of the end
you are where everything stopped making sense
you were the last month I saw myself alive

Dear August
you buckled my knees under a bloated moon
and watched me howl for him
you made a fool out of me
made me curse away the days
you made my teeth bite through my tongue
put a grit in all my greetings

Dear August
you humiliated me
I have creases in my cheeks now
from the nights that clot my memory
it all still rots in my brain
the faces blurred out

Dear August
my shins are still imbedded in the grass
there are half as many stars in the sky now
I don't dream of having a daughter anymore

Dear August
I think God put me together backwards

Dear August
my own blood is on my hands

....

Dear August
I made it to September

Main Street

when I left you
I found myself
in the middle of Main street
right where I left my body
for the first time in months
I held her
for the first time in years
I chose her

figment

there is no longer a version of the story
where things end happily
it will never snow in the right seasons
as long as you are by my side
the only way to visit you
is in my nightmares
and I'm not willing to live
in that world anymore
I hate you more than I ever loved you
I loved a man who wore your face
but lied about his soul
would've given up an arm to be chosen by
the beauty I saw
would've jumped if you asked me in July
because I swore one night
the man I made up in my head lived in you
now it's January and you're nothing to me
I scribbled your jawline crooked
We are a finished story and I don't want to remember the details
just want to remember the legs that run
the farther I get, the more ordinary you look
more holes are in the ceiling we slept under
this poem is addressed
to a man who never really existed

recovery

one day, the morning was marinated in caramel
the clocks were pumice stone
grating the trauma into fine sand to fall through my fingers
the swings swayed through teal sky
blowing kisses from the clouds

      and nothing hurt anymore

the forgotten body
empty pill bottles
the sheets pulled over my head all winter
it was all just a distant memory
not an artery
not a lesion
but a lesson
that fits into the grooves of my palm
builds tissue strong enough
to grow a million arms in place of the harm
and hold myself into eternity

a letter to myself

I'm sorry
he made you feel like you're hard to love
I'm sorry you're afraid to try again
but for what it's worth
I've loved you
all the days he couldn't
I've pushed oxygen through your lungs
I've pulled the sun into the sky for you
I've planted seeds in your scars
to grow new armor
I've loved you
and it isn't hard
it is beautiful
it is my purpose

dear everything
that tried to kill me
you have beautifully
and wonderfully
Failed

"dear everything
that tried to kill me
you have beautifully
and wonderfully
failed"

Mom's story

i.

In several languages, Linda means beautiful
in its Germanic roots it means soft or tender
in the language of your daughters
it means the keeper of light
the first warm chest to meet our cheeks
the woman who weaved safety into newborn skin
daughter of Italian immigrant Adua Pagliocca Voci
wading her way into America smelling of the streets of Naples
with Italian tongue tying over the English she pressed against her tongue
Nana was just finding her footing here when she became your mother
so little Linda read bedtime stories to herself
could not ask for help on homework
could not fill her tummy at dinner time
I wonder if this is where you learned to do it all yourself
daughters are not a delicacy in Italian households

ii.

she was never a good mother
but you remained a great daughter
you have been the only person who's stayed
you now change your own mother's diapers
is that not the most profound act of love
to care for the mother who never mothered you
to hold her in her most vulnerable state
to forgive her for all the ways she failed you
to wait 58 years to hear your mother tell you she loves you
you became the best mother without ever seeing the blueprint

iii.

there were years I did not know how to be your daughter
you were never given the space to fall apart in emotion
you told me you never cried over a boy
never combusted under the weight of life
then you birthed me
a young girl swimming in tears

engulfed in the complex world spinning in her head
you had to find the words to guide me through it
you sat at the edge of my bed through the night
just to make sure I made it to the morning
pressed thumbs against my severed skin
wrapped gauze around a child you could not understand
still loved me when I was a black cloud hanging in the living room
when I rained for years because I was granted a home safe enough to do so

iv.
Mom, I'm sorry for who I was in my darkest moments.
I hope when you look into the night sky,
the stars hug you tight enough to reach your younger self
I hope little Linda is in awe of all you've become despite all you were up
against
I hope you are proud when you reflect on the relationship your three
daughters have with you
our love for you is a testament to your lifelong work as a mother, friend, and
hero

v.
we are made of you
we are the home cooked meal
after a day of breastfeeding alone while two toddlers littered the wooden
floors
we are the clean sheets you stretched around our mattress
before bedtime while we scrambled to finish our homework
we are the filled up gas tank before a long day on the road back to UMass
we are the puppy you brought home for Christmas in 2007
we are the cheerleader in the bleachers of every basketball game
to be made of you is to be life's most sacred magic trick
is to house an inextinguishable love
I wish for every corner of your life to wrap its arms around you
I wish for you to be held through the night
I wish you rest
I wish you sushi and red wine
I wish you sundresses and sand that burns your toes
I wish you a thousand pink skies
and I wish to remind you everyday
that to have a mother like you is a miracle

a woman like me

the town would lose its footing
in a woman like me
there is a canine sharpness
about my laughter
a parading city in my joy
the power I possess
swirled in barbed wire
you want to melt me down to broth
so your masculinity has a fighting chance
you're the kind of guy who calls women bitches
expects us to choke on your oversized ego and spit you out whole
you're the kind of boy who thinks he can walk in and out of my body
planting seeds until you grow into a man
but I am not made of second chances
I save those for myself
what a divine intervention it is that men like you
don't want women like me
I eat men like you off the bone
devour flesh
as its own home-cooked meal
wasn't your first home a womb?
you have a brain that cannot fathom me
my magic is not meant to meet your shadow
this body is lifted with a thousand leathered hands
reincarnated with my Nana's nose and my mother's brow
my grandmother's grace
I am a mosaic of my ancestors who broke free from men like you
women who walked so I could run
who pushed out a universe from between their legs
and you think you're clever, using the most powerful organ as your baseless
punchline
you think degrading me will disintegrate my pedestal
foolish boy, playing with a poet's pen
don't you know a man like you
will never prevail over a woman like me

the color of tomorrow

since I could not matter to you
I turned the lights off
in every room I unlocked for you
I set that world afire
the one where the sun only rose when you came around
the one I painted your favorite color
that still wasn't enough
I let the layer of skin you touched
turn to ash
now when I think of you
I smell burning buildings
now that you're gone
the grass is growing back
now that I'm mine again
I matter enough to myself
there is no room for you
no one can make the sky fall anymore
the sun doesn't need to be begged out the clouds
it just shines

to the retrograde

the thing about the things that don't kill you
is they stay in the cemetery of your stomach
living an afterlife inside you
and on the bad days
they climb up your rock wall lungs
remind every molecule of the weight your marrow carries
but the thing about the things that don't kill you
is they are no longer scary
the bad days have proven to not be fatal
the thing about surviving is I lived to see the sun rise again
everything that has ruined me
I've made a mountain out of
and watched the sunset from its peak
so I write a letter to the retrograde
and to the woman
with the worn body
who rose despite the casualties, ruminating
I tell her
you are not the blackened sky
you are not the night you split yourself in two
you are not the darkest hour
that gave herself up for liar telling the love story
you are poet pulling herself from the poison even in the fiercest belly of the
sea
you are every color of earth
even your madness deserves to be held
you are universe
not simply typhoon
still greenhouse
still gravel heart
still standing
despite all odds

homecoming

all my love letters
have learned to walk their way back to me
my body
a homecoming hyperbole
a rebellion of rage
laying like massacre
screaming like sacrament
like demand
like
let's be everything they took away from us
let's be all our ugly
let's let our necks grow crooked
graffiti their expectations
mud pool in the plastic
you will not bypass my kingdom
you will not dispose of what was never yours
your footprints will not last more than a moment
everything I thought I loved about you
was only my own light circling back to me

Lafayette Street

I think my neighbors are falling in love
they spent the whole night playing star and moon
on the roof of the pizza shop our apartment windows peer onto
dangling bare feet over Lafayette street
making constellations with conversations
head nesting into shoulder
I watch their two play-dough bodies melt into one
I didn't tell them, they kept me up all night
they deserve to fall in love loudly
they deserve to come inside on their own time
I don't blame them for using the sky as a blanket
I don't blame them for filling the hallway with marijuana smoke
for emptying the tinted wine bottle
engraving their name into the stucco
I don't blame them for writing a story mid air
and letting it stay there
I'm sure everyone in the neighborhood
can recite their midnight conversations
we've all let the soundtrack of their becoming
sit on our windowsills
I don't mind the welding of a newborn love
it reminds me of what I've lost
it reminds me of what's to come

esperanza

you are a newborn morning
I pull tired out of bed
you build a castle in the sky
make broken things fly
for the thousandth time
your miracles never get old

galactic girl

you are a poet
stop coating your fires in sugar
stop making yourself smaller
for hands that don't deserve to hold you
you were not made to fulfill
someone else's idea of beautiful
you were made with
a milky way tongue
let them tremble
you are a woman
let them worship
go ahead
be loudly unimpressed
let your boundaries grow fangs
you are not convenience
you are not free entrance
let your standards scare
them away
they never belonged here anyway

it's not too late to start a garden in a graveyard

I stopped having a brain that eats itself for dinner
no longer attending
the rehearsals
to self destruction

reclaiming a place in the sun

I've learned I'll survive
I'll survive being sad
someday I'll love again sad
I'll publish a book sad
I'll write this poem sad
I'll fight for you, sad
I'll keep trying to change the world, sad
I'll be alive and I'll laugh
I'll be sad
and I'll still do everything they do
while sad
I'll make it all the way
to that place in the sun
and it won't matter if I'm sad
because I'll have survived
because I'll have become her
this sad miracle
this galaxy of depression
this body so equipped to keep living

author bio

Olivia Laughlin is a fierce poet, artist and house of stories craving release through creative expression. Her work has been published in a multitude of journals and websites including Gabby & Min's Literary Review, The Radical Notion, SoulLit, and Wingless Dreamer. She has been featured in interviews published with Bold Journey and Canvas Rebel, delving into her artistry. Her inspiration is derived from the experiences that have ruptured her core and opened a portal of new becoming.

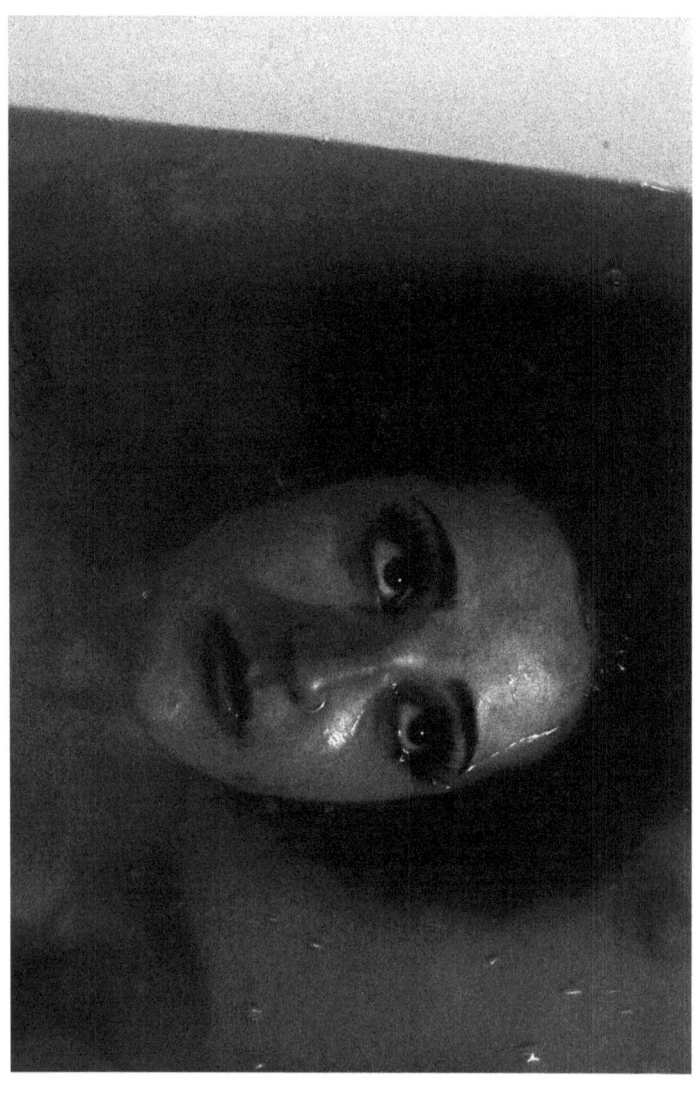

www.ingramcontent.com/pod-product-compliance
Lightning Source LLC
Chambersburg PA
CBHW040856120626
46551CB00001B/38

*9 7 9 8 9 9 9 1 6 5 0 1 5 *